Deception Detection

A Pocket Guide to Statement Analysis, Micro-expressions, Body Language, Interviews and Interrogations

By Daniel E. Loeb, M.A.

Deception Detection: A Pocket Guide to Statement
Analysis, Micro-expressions, Body Language,
Interviews and Interrogations

By Daniel E. Loeb

Copyright © 2014

ISBN-13: 978-1494834876   ISBN-10: 1494834871

TABLE OF CONTENTS

– Foreword –

The Deception Detection guidebook is not intended to provide a thorough explanation of the various concepts involved in Statement Analysis, Body Language, or Deception Detection. This handbook is intended to be used as a reference for supervisors, Law Enforcement Officers, or other deception detectors to quickly refresh or review the various concepts. This guide is not written in a chapter format, but seeks to provide a quick overview of the various concepts/topics and to provide the reader with the gist of the information. It is meant to be a small handy guidebook that can fit in one's pocket; giving access to the desired information without the need to sift through long case studies or filibustered material in order to review/recall the basic principles.

6 Deception Detection

The Truth, Whole Truth, and Nothing but the Truth

The Truth (a person may provide false information)

The Whole Truth (a person may be truthful, but omit critical information)

Nothing but the Truth (a person may evade/avoid answering questions)

The truth alone would not suffice, because someone can also deceive by telling the truth yet leaving out critical information. Besides refusing to tell the truth or the whole truth, a person may also attempt to deceive by evading a direct question by providing irrelevant information (something other than the truth).

Lies, Perfidy, Tactical Deception

Ruses of war are legitimate so long as they do not involve treachery or perfidy on the part of the belligerent resorting to them...Treacherous or perfidious conduct in war is forbidden because it destroys the basis for a restoration of peace short of the complete annihilation of one belligerent by the other. — FM 27-10 (Law of Land Warfare), Chapter 2, 50

Who do you owe the truth to?
(Not to Enemies/predators/strangers)

Military/Business Ethics
(Needed for maintaining trust)

Pro-Social Lying
(Social lubricant/Equivocation/White Lies)

Anti-Social Lying
(Spreading false rumors/concealing guilt)

Not all lies are bad, some are social lubricant (providing expected answers to questions such as "How are you doing today?"), and other lies are required for one's personal safety (not giving a bad guy information to use against you).

Evaluating Deception

Look for Hot Spots/sensitive areas or subjects that cause the person to change their behavior, become nervous, or otherwise divert from their baseline.

Does the person have a motivation to lie?

Examine the situation from an outsider's perspective. If an outsider would not accept/believe it, you shouldn't either.

Listen to the sentence structure: are sentences fragmented?

Are their unnecessary words added to a sentence? If so, it was done for a reason.

Is the person providing too much detail – in an effort to make his story sound more believable?

Is the person providing an unsolicited alibi? Is he providing an explanation of his behavior prior to be asked a question?

Is the person's story feasible, does it make sense?

Is the story proportional? Not missing information in the beginning, middle, or end.

Is the person answering the question that was asked?

Is there a delay in his response?

Spoken Words

Literal Words, Emotions, Emphasis, and Inflection, how things are said can change their meaning. (Dillingham, 2008)

- I <u>like</u> you (more than just a little bit)

- <u>I</u> like you (everyone else probably doesn't)

- I like <u>you </u>(probably doesn't like everyone else though)

- <u>I</u> like <u>you</u>? (sarcasm/not likely)

Statement Analysis

The shortest sentence is usually the best sentence. Any additional or unnecessary words added to a sentence are relevant, and may provide you with significant information.

Look for lengthy sentences, and try to shorten them. Any extra words added to a sentence may provide you with further insight into the person, situation, or motives.

"*I don't know for sure anything about what's going on at all*" - Tonya Harding, 11 January 1994

Shortened, "I don't know what's going on."

Extra words: for sure, anything, at all

"*I don't know for sure anything about what's going on at all*" - Tonya Harding, 11 January 1994

"*For Sure*" is a qualifier, used to provide the speaker with a way out – should her deception be uncovered. Since she was not 'sure' of the validity of her answer, any response cannot be trusted as being accurate/valid.

"*I don't know for sure anything about what's going on at all*" - Tonya Harding, 11 January 1994

"Anything" is an overemphasis or exaggeration. She likely had some general knowledge of the event/subject, or people wouldn't be asking her questions.

"I don't know for sure anything about what's going on at all" - Tonya Harding, 11 January 1994

"At All" is an overemphasis or exaggeration used to convince the hearer of something. 'At All' is an absolute, which is rarely warranted. A truthful person usually does not feel the need to add qualifiers or exaggerations to their statements in order to convince the hearer of the trustworthiness of their statement.

Qualifiers

Qualifiers are used to make a statement sound more believable. A deceptive person may use qualifiers, which he/she believes makes his/her statement sound more credible, or the person may use them to express a lack of certainty in their statement.

"I swear", "with God as my witness", "as a Christian", "To tell you the truth", "Honestly", "Frankly", "Actually", "Really", "I think", "I believe", "I don't recall", "I can't be sure, but..."

A truthful person usually doesn't feel the need to qualify his/her statements. When seeking the truth or conducting an investigation, you want the facts. You are looking for just the facts, not maybes, uncertainties, or speculations. A vague statement full of uncertainties does not provide you with evidence you can corroborate.

Leakage

The truth may slip out through emotional responses (such as micro-expressions), unusual words or phrases, body language, or sentence structure.

Everything a person says has a meaning, and the person means what he/she says. Pay attention to the word choices a person makes. If a word choice seems odd, think about the definition of the word, and try to determine if there is a reason the person used it.

Look for fragmented sentences, and ask yourself what the person left out. What could the person have been thinking about that distracted him to the point that he could no longer construct a sentence?

What topic was being discussed?

Did the person stop himself to avoid revealing something?

Is he leaving something out of the sentence, if so why?

Grammar Usage

Pay attention to grammar usage and unique words. Pay particular attention to how the words: 'Never', 'Actually', and 'With' are used.

'Never' means 'Not Ever', it does not mean 'No.'

If someone uses the word 'Never' in place of 'No' then they may be attempting to deceive you. If asked a direct question, a truthful person should provide a direct answer. Anything else is an attempt to avoid answering the question.

'Actually' is used to compare two thoughts. If a question does not require the person to compare one action to another, then the word 'Actually' should not be in the answer – unless the person is comparing a truthful response to the one they 'actually' decide to provide.

The word 'With' implies distance, which may or may not be warranted. (Dillingham, 2008)

"I went out to eat with my wife."

"My wife and I went out to eat."

"Me and Jane went out to eat."

"We got something to eat."

The word 'With' implies distance, which may or may not be warranted.

"*I went out to eat with my wife.*"
(The person separates/distances himself (I) from his wife as much as the sentence will allow) (Dillingham, 2008)

"*My wife and I went out to eat.*"
(Spoken more formally, but implies more of a joint venture)

"*Me and Jane went out to eat.*"
(More relaxed and personable, and implies a joint venture)

"*We went out to eat.*"
(Implies a partnership)

By examining the sentence structure and word choices, you can get a glimpse of how the person felt about the experience. Was he not pleased to be there, did so out of a felt obligation, a relaxed and personable experience, or a partnership?

Closeness or Distance

(This, That, These, Those)

Are the above words used correctly in a sentence/statement?

'This' and 'These' represent closeness.

'That' and 'Those' represent distance.

Is the person trying to distance himself from his actions, or expressing closeness/familiarity that shouldn't be there?

"*I was walking to my car when 'this' man...*"

Why does the speaker use the word 'this' in the above sentence? 'This' implies closeness.

Does the person know the man?

Is the man a fictional representation of the speaker, which might explain why the speaker feels a sense of closeness to the character?

When introducing a new person or object to a discussion, the indefinite article is used first, and any further references use the definite article ('a' man, followed by 'the' man).

Definite or Indefinite Articles

Pay attention to the usage of the 'Definite' and 'Indefinite' articles in sentences. A person should introduce a person or object using the indefinite article, and then use the definite article thereafter.

If a person introduces an object using the definite article, then at least in the person's mind, the person/object has already been introduced or is known to the speaker.

"I entered the building and the man grabbed me."

Active or Passive Voice

At that point: "*I fired the gun.*"
(Active voice: takes responsibility for the actions)

"*The gun went off*"
(Distancing language: the inanimate object fired itself/removing personal responsibility)

"*A shot rang out*"
(Distancing language: implying that the speaker isn't even sure which gun fired)

Pronouns

(I, Us, We, They)

Pronouns give us responsibility. In an effort to avoid responsibility, or blame, a person might use plural pronouns to share the blame with others.

If other people are not involved, a person should not refer to himself in the plural. Talking about oneself in the third person would also be suspicious.

"*I thought we had a plan to avoid such mistakes. You try to avoid stuff like this, but apparently, we failed this time.*"

"I thought we had a plan to avoid such mistakes. You try to avoid stuff like this, but apparently, we failed this time."

'I thought', the speaker doesn't take responsibility for anything other than 'thinking.' 'Mistakes' may be an attempt to minimize an offense or deliberate action. 'You try' speaks of something someone else does. 'Apparently' implies that the fact might not even be true, but might only appear to be. 'We failed' distances the speaker from personal responsibility, and shares the blame with others, who may not even exist.

'We'

The plural 'We' can be used to reduce personal responsibility or it can be used to demonstrate a partnership.

Should a partnership exist in the statement/sentence?

Is the person attempting to reduce his role in the event, or is he demonstrating a partnership that shouldn't be there?

"He forced me into his car, and <u>we</u> drove to ..."

"He forced me into his car, and <u>drove me</u> to..."

Verb Tense

If a person is recalling an event, he should be speaking in the 'Past Tense.' Look for any 'Present Tense' statements added to a story, as they might indicate the person is constructing the events 'presently.'

Alternately, if a person is speaking of an ongoing event, but uses the 'past tense', that too may be a clue to deception.

"*I am deeply concerned about the missing child; he <u>was</u> such a great kid.*"

"<u>*Sprinting*</u> *across the street, I noticed a car had crashed into...*"

When people are retrieving information from their memories, they usually speak in the Past Tense. Since deceptive people are fabricating or modifying facts from truthful events, they may slip up and use the past or present tenses interchangeably.

Liars mentally rehearse their stories in the present tense. Once they are satisfied that their explanation sounds believable, they translate the present tense verbs into past tense verbs in order to simulate a truthful narrative. Due to the mental complexities involved, liars may mix up the present/past verbs, and subconsciously speak or write narratives using both past and present tense verbs. Verb tense changes are a clue to deception.

Expanded Contractions

People normally speak in contractions. However, deceptive people tend to speak more formally – because they are making a concerted effort to carefully choose their words – and thereby expand their contractions to emphasize clarity.

'I didn't' becomes *'I did not'*

Expanded Contractions demonstrate an overemphasis on clarity that may or may not be warranted. Honest people usually do not feel the need to add qualifiers, expand their contractions, or do anything else to convince the hearer of their truthfulness.

Listen for expanded contractions, such as, *'No, I did not."*

The simplest response to a 'Yes' or 'No' question is either 'Yes' or 'No.' Adding anything else to the statement is done for a reason, such as to convince the hearer of the person's certainty of the 'No' answer.

Responding to a Yes/No question with, *'No, I didn't'* is not necessary. If the person goes a step further by expanding his contractions to *'No, I did not'*, the phrase "*the lady doth protest too much*" may apply.

"I did not have sexual relations with that woman, Miss Lewinsky."

Personal Dictionary

One technique liars use to aid them in deception is to modify their 'Personal Dictionary', or to redefine words. This is similar to how a person might be able to avoid the stresses/pressure of outright lying by providing an honest response to a different question than the one that was asked.

Did you drink a beer?

"No." [I drank four beers, not one]

"I did not have <u>sexual relations</u> with that woman, Miss Lewinsky."

In regards to the above statement, President Clinton later stated that he did not include the act of receiving oral sex in his definition of '*Sexual Relations.*'

Modifying one's 'Personal Dictionary' allows deceptive people to provide truthful answers to different questions than what was asked of them. They rephrase the question in their own minds (differently) and/or change the definition of words in their responses without letting the questioner know that they've changed the meaning of their words.

Everyone has an internal dictionary. Some liars are able to change their internal definitions of words without notifying their intended targets.

Synonyms are another thing to be mindful of. People are usually consistent in their word usage. If the speaker switches the word he uses to describe something, there is usually a reason for it. If car becomes vehicle, girl becomes female, or money becomes currency, you may have identified a Hot Spot worthy of closer examination.

Statement Analysis Example

"*I did not have sexual relations with that woman, Miss Lewinsky.*"

I "did not" is an expanded contraction; a more formal manner of speaking with an emphasis on clarity.

"Sexual relations" was redefined in President Clinton's Personal Dictionary, so that it did not include Oral Sex in its definition.

"That" is Distancing Language.

"That woman" is also an attempt to distance himself from a woman whose first name he knew, and who he worked with often.

"Miss" is a more formal speech pattern, used when talking about strangers, and is usually not used to describe someone you know by name and/or had a relationship with (you wouldn't introduce your wife or grandmother as Miss Jones).

Minimization

Minimization is used to reduce the impact of an action, and to make it seem like it wasn't that big of a deal.

"I was only" or "I just", are attempts to reduce the importance of the event/action.

Euphemisms are used in an effort to say things more tactfully, such as when a beloved pet is "put to sleep."

Liars tend to minimize their actions so that they do not portray themselves in a bad light; 'Hurting' instead of 'killing', 'borrowing' instead of 'stealing.'

Truthful people are not afraid to say: murdered, killed, raped, stole, or any other such term, because they do not associate the punishment/consequences of the terms with themselves.

Diversion

Did the person answer the specific question asked?

Did he answer a question that wasn't asked?

Did he change the definition of a word or rephrase the question in order to answer a question that wasn't asked?

Is the person's answer relevant to the question?

Is the person attempting to change the subject, provide and evasive response, or respond to your question by asking you one?

Something Smells Fishy: A Red Herring is a logical fallacy meant to divert ones attention from the problem at hand. It is an attempt to distract the questioner from continuing in that line of questioning or to change the subject to something irrelevant.

Latency

Latency describes the time it takes for a person to respond to a question.

A liar needs to conceal and distort information in the story he is telling, while also adjusting his story to any new questions or evidence presented to him. He must conceal his emotions and present the information in a natural manner that does not cause suspicion. This requires a great deal of mental effort.

The higher the stakes of a lie, the more stressful and mentally challenging the process becomes. Do to all of the mental demands involved in deception; the dishonest person may take longer to respond to questions.

If a question is simply, such as, *"what is your name?"* The time required to respond should be minimal. If there is a big delay prior to answering a question, that is due to the person thinking and formulating a response – which may be a clue to deception.

To detect deception, ask yourself if the extra time is warranted in order to answer the question?

If it isn't, you may have identified a hot spot.

Latency may consist of long periods of silence, or the person may attempt to stall for time by asking you to repeat the question, or restating the question in their response.

"Did I take money from the stack fund? I am the last person you should be suspicious of, but to answer your question, No, I did not take any money from the snack fund or anything else."

Omission

Instead of providing false information that may be discovered, many deceptive people choose to 'Lie by Omission.'

The majority of their statements are comprised of the truth, so the amount of stress induced leakage is minimal, and the person's lie harder to detect.

To 'lie by omission', the person skips over or leaves out, key/critical pieces of information. They provide the truth, but they do not provide the whole truth.

Unless you have other sources of information, you do not know what the person does not tell you.

To avoid missing out on key points, look for words that span time being added to a statement, and inquire about the missing information.

'Afterwards', 'Later', 'Shortly thereafter', 'A few minutes later', 'the next thing I knew' etc...

Try to identify when information is skipped over or withheld, and focus your inquiry on obtaining the missing information.

Order

Most people will remain consistent with the order they list things. For example, people usually list/describe their children in order from oldest to youngest. If during a conversion, they change that practice, or start listing their kids in a different order, the person has a reason for doing so.

It may be that the person originally introduced his/her kids in chronological order by age, but as the topic of conversion changed to sports, the person may start listing the kids in order of athletic ability.

When a person is recalling events, it is usually in a narrative from start to finish. If the person starts adding things out of order, that may be a sign that they are fabricating the story.

"We left the house after lunch and went straight to Kevin's house. After working on the yard for an hour, we had to hurry to get ready for the game. When we were eating lunch, Kevin mentioned that he felt sick, which is why we were trying to get the yard worked done early...so we can make it to the game on time."

Proportionate Stories

When people recall events, they include a proportionate amount of background information, describe the main event, and then describe what took place afterwards.

Generally, people will devote 25% of their stories to pre-incident, 50% to the event, and 25% to what happened afterwards.

Any significant divergence from those proportions should cause you to be suspicious of deception.

The portions of a person's story may not be 25/50/25, but they should at least contain a before, during, and after.

If someone provides an enormous amount of background information, skips over the main event, and then provides information that occurred afterwards, the person is probably keeping things from you, and lying by omission.

If a person describes the main event, but lacks detail regarding the before or after portions of the story, that might also be a clue that the story is made up. When fabricating a story, the liar anticipates what he/she believes the investigator will focus on. The liar rehearses his/her story, and constructs what he/she determines to be believable. The liar focuses on what he/she thinks he will be questioned about, and may lack details in the other aspects of his/her story. Inquiring about those sections of the alibi, may stump the liar, as he/she may not have predetermined responses available.

When a liar fabricates a story, he/she rehearses it in a certain order, and must alter/modify the story to account for any new information the investigator presents or discovers during questioning.

Asking the person to retell their story from different parts of the story, or in a different order, may cause the dishonest person to slip up. If a person is telling you the truth, aside from reliving a traumatic event, an honest person should not have any difficulty recounting events from any timeframe of the story, because the truth doesn't change.

Christopher Dillingham suggests counting the number of lines in the Before, During, and After segments of a written statement, and then multiplying each amount by 100, and then dividing that number by the total number of sentences, in order to get the percentages of each segment of a statement and suggests the following percentages as a gauge:

Segments	Truthful	Deceptive
Before	25%	35%
During	50%	50%
After	25%	15%

The Number 3

Christopher Dillingham also suggests listening for the number 3 in statements.

Many fictional stories use the number 3 in them, such as *'the Three Little Pigs'*, or *'Goldilocks and the Three Bears.'* So when people need to make up a fictional number, deceptive people tend to use the number 3 (perhaps subconsciously), and claim there were three robbers, it was around 3 o'clock, they lost 3 hundred dollars, etc...

Establishing a Baseline

There isn't a universal way to determine if someone is lying, the best we can do is to identify 'Hot Spots.'

'Hot Spots' refer to sections of a person's story, or responses to certain topics that differ from the norm.

Hot Spots are detected by noticing changes in a person's 'Baseline' behavior. Before you can recognize changes in a person's baseline behavior, you must first determine how a person normally responds. This is the same procedure used in polygraph examinations.

Polygraphs measure physical changes in a person's body in response to questioning, and compare that information to the baseline responses observed during the non-stressful questions.

Baseline questions usually consist of demographic information, such as a person's name, address, or other information that are not stressful to answer.

Once a baseline has been established, unexplained changes from the norm may aid the questioner in identifying Hot Spots, or topics that are 'sensitive' to the interviewee.

If a person normally speaks with his hands (uses illustrators) or at certain speed/rate, uses certain words/emotions, or demonstrates other behaviors while engaged in a normal conversation, but changes his behavior in response to certain questions or topics that can be a clue to help the interviewer uncover sensitive topics/areas for the person.

Deceptive people tend to diminish their movements (use less illustrators), because they are attempting to control so much of their body language and grooming behaviors in an effort to prevent leakage.

Behavioural Profiling

Behavior Profilers use a similar technique, by looking for unusual behavior, which differs from the norm.

At a checkpoint, a profiler may offer the same greeting to hundreds of people, and will probably receive one of only a dozen or so responses.

If a person responds in an unusual manner, that is a clue that the person may need to be subjected to additional scrutiny.

If asked, *"How are you doing?"* and the normal response is for someone to acknowledge the question and provide a short answer, that could be used as a 'Baseline' response.

If a person responds by providing a long and detailed response containing unnecessary information, that person may require more questioning.

If someone locks up their body parts, appears nervous, ignores the question, and looks straight ahead while trying to speed through security, that person may require additional scrutiny.

If asked, *"How are you doing?"* and the person turns around and starts running away, that is reasonably suspicion to investigate the person. If in response to a greeting, a person assumes a defensive posture, clenches his fists, and prepares to fight, that response too would be out of the norm.

Changes from the Baseline

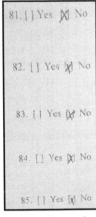

In order to recognize changes in a person's baseline, you must first determine how the person behaves normally. Once a baseline has been established, any significant change in a person's behavior may indicate an emotional response, or hot spot, to a certain stimuli.

In this example, a baseline is established by observing the manner in which a person marked his Xs on a questionnaire. When asked if the person used illegal drugs, his X is significantly different from his baseline. Notice out the X in the below example does not touch any of the sides of the box. Such as response does not mean the person is lying or is an illegal drug user, but it does represent that the person experienced a behavioral change in response to the question. Maybe the person has strong feelings about illegal drug use even though he does not use them, or the person may have experienced a feeling of shame, which caused him to make his X as small as possible in an effort to have this area of his life overlooked.

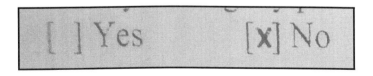

Higher Pitched or Breaking Voice

When people become nervous, physiological changes take place in their bodies, which cause them to speak in a higher pitched voice, or may cause them to have trouble speaking, such as stuttering or causing their voice to break.

When people get excited, they also speak faster (speech rate).

The above is true of both honest and dishonest people. If observed, the interviewer will need to determine if the response is warranted/legitimate, or if it is a clue to deception.

Does the person have a reason to be scared, or is the person scared of getting caught in a lie?

The Eyes

There is a myth that liars can't *'look you in the eye'*, or *'say it to your face.'*

Liars too are aware of this myth, and will often make an extra effort to ensure they are looking directly into your eyes when they lie to you.

The amount of eye contact, blink rate, or whether the person looks up, down, left, or right in response to questions are not indicators of deception. They only provide 'Hot Spots', if the behavior differs significantly from the person's 'Baseline' behavior.

Body Language

Shoulder Shrugs usually accompany uncertain statements, such as when a person is saying, *"I don't know'*, or *'I don't care.'*

Shoulder shrugs may be a subconscious response associated with a person's affirmative statement.

If a person says, *"I don't know"*, accompanied by a shoulder shrug, that is an appropriate response.

If a person says, *"I have never been to that side of town"*, with an accompanying shoulder shrug that may be Leakage.

If the person's action/behavior is not consistent with his/her statement (the body says, *"I don't know"*, while the mouth says, *"This is a fact")*, then you must ask yourself if there is a legitimate reason for that response.

Is the person making a denial while thinking to himself, *'I don't know - if you will believe me'*, or is he making a statement he isn't sure about?

Much has been said in popular culture about open or closed body postures. Claims that if a person has his arms crossed or folded then that is supposed to mean that the person is subconsciously trying to block you out or shell up, while an open body posture is supposed to mean the person is being open and inviting towards you.

There is both truth and myth to the above. The bottom line is that there isn't a universal meaning that is always correct. A person might fold his arms because he is bored or cold or he may be trying to block you out or protect his vital organs.

To determine if you have identified a Hot Spot, the behavior must differ from the person's baseline.

Grooming and nervous movements/behaviors may also provide leakage or clues to deception, if they differ from the person's baseline.

Grooming involves scratching, combing hair, picking at fingernails, picking lent, rubbing eyes, whipping nose, yawning, stretching, and other self-care related activities. If you are a suspect in an armed robbery and someone asks you why your car was observed speeding away from the scene of the crime, that is not the time to start tying your shoes or cleaning out your ears.

Nervous movements might include shaking (of the legs or other body parts), blushing, twiddling of the thumbs, etc...

Grooming and nervous movements are only clues to deception if they differ from the person's normal behavior (baseline).

If they do differ from the person's baseline, you must ask yourself why they do. Is the behavior explainable under the circumstances?

'Congruence' refers to whether or not a person's emotions and/or body language match the person's statements.

Shoulder Shrugs and head nods/shakes (yes/no) are emblems. 'Emblems' should be congruent with a person's statements.

If a person makes a factual statement while shrugging his/her shoulders, or say 'yes' while shaking his/her head 'no', the lack of congruence may provide you with reason to explore the topic in more detail.

Posture

Defensive postures can also be identified while a person is sitting down. If a person's shoulders are not squared up to yours, the person may be assuming a defensive posture (like the fighting position of a standing person).

They may also lean back in their chair to get as far away from the interviewer as possible, move their chair, sit sideways, or cross their legs (with a raised knee) or fold their arms to protect their abdomen (a perceived vulnerable area).

When a person's shoulders slouch and his/her head drops forward in a defeated position, the person may be ready to give up and might be close to making a confession.

Micro-Expressions

Micro-Expressions are subconscious expressions of emotions that last for approximately $1/15^{th}$ of a second.

They are uncontrolled expressions of emotion, which a deceptive person may be unable to prevent.

During a conversation, a person may wait until it is his turn to speak, but our emotional responses do not wait for an appropriate time to be expressed. If someone imagines a horrible smell or a disgusting image, the person may display a micro-expression of disgust, regardless of whether or not they say, *"That is gross!"*

The timing of emotional displays is also important.

The emotion usually comes first. If someone slams his hand down against a table and then simulates an angry expression that is an example of inappropriate emotional response – the person should get angry prior to acting angry.

The expression of surprise should only last a moment.

If an emotion seems prolonged or occurring only after an action, then the emotion is probably being faked.

Emotions usually precede physical and/or verbal actions.

The fact that a micro-expression occurs, does not

automatically mean the person is lying; it just means that the person experienced an emotional response to certain stimuli. If you observe a micro-expression, you must ask yourself:

Did a micro-expression occur?

Did you see a conflicting emotion?
(Did the person state, "Me and Susan are great friends" while displaying a look of anger or disgust?)

Is there a reason for the emotional response? Test your hypotheses by asking more questions on the related topic.

Micro-expressions provide emotional clues, but you must ask yourself, *"is the person lying about his feelings, or responding to his feelings about lying."* Once you identify a micro-expression, you must determine if the emotion is appropriate, conflicting, or why the person experienced it.

'Lying about feelings': claiming to be very sad or worried about their missing co-worker, while flashing periodic expressions of happiness and joy.

'Feelings about lying': the person may feel guilty about lying, may feel fear he will get caught in the lie, or may have duping delight (get pleasure out of deceiving you). According to Matsumoto, there are 7 Basic Emotions that may be identified during a Micro-Expression. Joy, Surprise, Contempt, Sadness, Anger, Disgust, Fear.

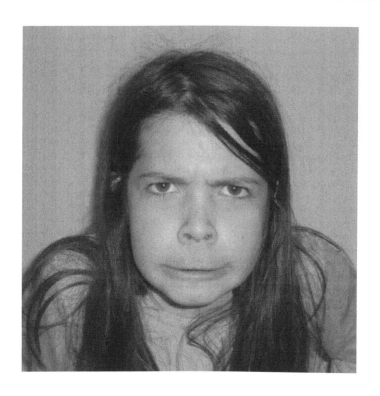

Anger: brows down and together, upper eyelid rose (giving staring or glaring quality), Lower eyelid tensed, lips tightened or pursed. Associated Nonverbal Behavior (NVB): Posture: head and chin forward. Voice: Edge, harsh, loud. Triggers: goal obstruction, perceptions of injustice, norm violations.

Contempt: eyes neutral. Lip corner tightened and/or pulled up on only one side (smirk), one-sided (asymmetric) smile or smirk. Associated NVB: Posture: head back and sideways, looking down his/her nose. Voice: smug sounds. Triggers: immoral actions.

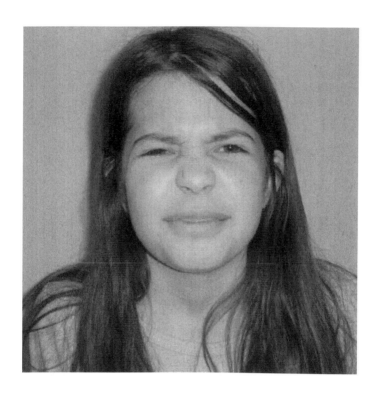

Disgust: wrinkling of the nose (eyebrows pulled down because of that), raising the upper lip, mouth can be open or closed, lips loose. Associated NVB: Posture: turning away. Voice: yuck sounds. Triggers: offensive objects, contamination.

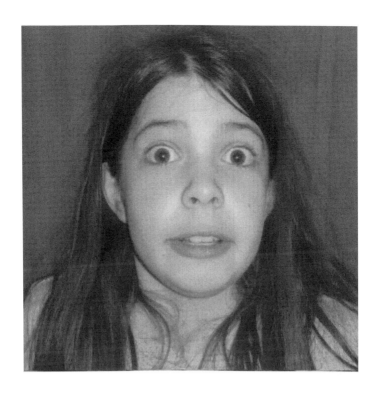

Fear: brows pulled up but may also be pulled together, often producing horizontal, wavy lines across the forehead. Upper eyelid tensed. Lips stretched horizontally. Associated NVB: Posture: head and body back; freezing or moving away. Voice: higher pitch, sudden inhalations. Triggers: threat of hard to self or well-being.

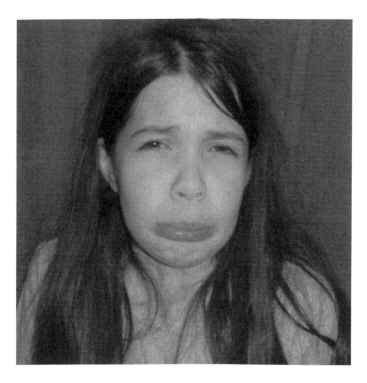

Sadness: inner corners of eyebrows raised, eyes loose,
upper eyelid drooping, lip corners pulled down.
Associated NVB: Posture: head and eyes down; loss
of muscle tone. Voice: softer, less words. Triggers:
love of loved object, distress.

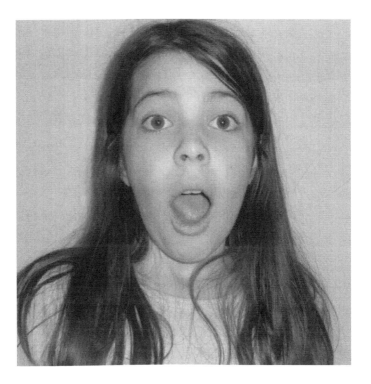

Surprise: brows rose, upper eyelid raised just a little. Jaw dropped; mouth open. Associated NVB: Posture: shoulders up, Voice: raising voice, inhalation, ooh sounds. Triggers: sudden, unexpected, wow events.

Happiness: lip corners pulled up in a smile. Muscles around the eyes tightened, giving eyes a twinkle and reducing area in eye cover fold. Often raises cheeks, producing shiny area. Associated NVB: Posture: receptive, approaching. Voice: enthusiastic, approaching. Triggers: goal attainment, self-satisfaction, pleasurable sensations.

Genuine smiles have wrinkles in the eyes; otherwise they are asymmetrical. When greeting someone, raised eyebrows (happy surprise) may also demonstrate that the person is actually happy to see you, & not merely providing you with a polite smile.

Manipulative Techniques

Though not directly related to detecting deception, having an understanding of manipulative techniques, may aid the interviewer in identifying a manipulative person's strategy. (Simon, 2010)

When dealing with manipulative people: accept no excuses, judge actions not intentions, and remind yourself of the facts involved (These are the facts…).

'Guilt-tripping': involves trying to make a person feel guilty about something in order to pressure them into giving into the manipulator. (You owe me)

'Shaming': uses subtle sarcasm to shame the person into doing something. (Good mothers would ensure their children had new shoes every year)

'Projecting the Blame': involves finding scapegoats to blame the person's behavior on. (The devil made me do it)

'Going on the offensive': attacking the other person when confronted. (I can't believe you of all people would accuse me of this, you are the one who…)

'Playing the victim': attempting to get sympathy or compassion. (I always fail like this; I can never do anything right)

'Denial': claiming ignorance (I don't know you're your talking about, I did not do it)

'Selective Inattention': ignoring anything that doesn't fit into the person's agenda. (The person simply ignores the aspects they are confronted with that they are clearly guilty of, and chooses topics to argue that are in their favor)

'Rationalization': justifying or excusing the person's behavior. (I was only/just doing what everyone else does)

'Evasion': providing vague or irrelevant responses to direct questions. (That doesn't really sound like me)

'Diversion': a moving target is hard to hit. The person attempts to change the subject or provide a red herring.

'Covert Intimidation': uses veiled threats to put the other person on the defensive or abandon their questioning. (I don't want us to be the kind of couple that gets a divorce after years of marriage, because one of the parties won't stop nagging the other)

'Vilifying the Victim': plays the victim and claims to have only responded to an attack – places the other person on the defensive. (I wouldn't have done anything if he didn't first accuse me of…)

'Playing the Role of the Servant': the person tries to excuse his/her behavior by acting as though they were working hard at serving a noble cause when really they are pursuing their own ambitions. (Of course I value this relationship, but I have a duty to God/work/community that sometimes must take priority).

'Seduction': praising, flattering, or charming in order to get what they want.

'Feigning Innocence': attempts to convince you that any harm the person caused was unintentional.

'Feigning Confusion': acting like he/she doesn't know what you are talking about, or is confused by one of your points.

'Feigning Outrage/Brandishing Anger': attempts to coerce or put the other person on the defensive.

'Overly helpful': an honest person will usually offer up information he/she believes will be helpful to the investigation – because they have nothing to hide – but be careful of the person who seems overly helpful. It may be a ploy to make the person seem innocent, or done in hopes of gaining the favor of the interviewer in case the deceiver is discovered later. It might be the person wants to get involved in the investigation in order to lead investigators down the wrong path.

'Unsolicited/Premature Excuses': prior to or at the start of an interview, a deceptive person might go into his/her pre-rehearsed alibi or excuse. A truthful person will not feel the need to provide such information until asked. However, a deceptive person who has planned out a strategy may want to get his/her story out there as quickly as possible.

'Focusing on Irrelevant Points': a deceptive person

might find one point in a case against him that is actually incorrect, and then focus on that one area, hoping that by proving it wrong, the investigation against him will be halted.

Persuasion

When seeking the truth, the interrogator may benefit from the use of persuasive techniques, such as:

'Appear to Authority/Power' (dressed in a power suit)

'Reciprocity' (makes the person feel obligated)

'Scarcity' (act now/limited time offer)

'Mirroring' (copying/mimicking the person's behavior/builds false rapport/we are the same)

'Interested is Interesting' (listen to person talk about themselves/they feel they've shared something with you/rapport building)

'Get a Small concession' (slowly convince the person to cross the Rubicon)

'Bandwagon' (everyone is doing it)

'Appeal to the Emotions' (present an emotional argument)

'Accuse the person of something worse' (people would rather admit to a lesser offense than to be blamed for something bigger that they didn't do). At some point state, *"I know there's something you haven't told me."* (Hoping they will offer up the missing information) Allow long periods of uncomfortable silence, which may cause them to talk in order to fill in the space.

Interviews and Interrogations

Interviews: are conducted in order to gain a better understanding of events. They are an attempt to gather information, and/or to put the pieces of a puzzle together. Interviews are conducted in order to obtain facts and information that can later be corroborated during an investigation.

Interrogations: are conducted after an investigation – in an effort to solicit a confession. Usually after having conducted multiple interviews and having obtained evidence establishing a person's guilt that the person will be confronted with.

During either an interview or an interrogation, the subject will probably have a pre-rehearsed story that he wants to tell. Let him tell the full story, and then ask questions to shoot holes in the story or to find inconsistencies.

When deceivers present a rehearsed story, they have constructed it from start to finish. If a story is fabricated, it is difficult for the deceiver to remain consistent when asked to retell the story in a different order or to start from a different point.

Lies are usually interwoven with the truth in order to reduce the amount of fictional information the liar needs to remember.

The liar may tell the truth for the most part, but may omit key information. Lying through omission or avoiding providing the whole truth reduces the chances of the lie being detected due to it conflicting with known facts.

Listen to the person's rehearsed story.

Identify and point out deception.

Look for motivations and justifications.

If you determine the person is lying/guilty, switch from an Interview to an Interrogation, and convince the person you know he/she is lying.

'Tactical Deception' is appropriate to use in order to obtain confessions from criminals. Claim to have witnesses, claim there is security camera footage, or phone recordings. Display a folder full of papers to give the appearance of a thorough investigation – the liar does not know what you know or what you do not know, but he must adjust his story to match or explain away any new information you present).

After shooting holes in the person's story and convincing him that you know he is lying, offer the person a way out, and an incentive to confess.

Once the subject is demonstrating defeated body language (shoulders dropped, head hanging in shame), you will accuse him of lying/the act.

You may need to overcome his denials/barriers, before you can move on to theme development.

In order to obtain the Truth or a Confession, you will

need to give the person a reason to provide you with the information.

No one confesses without having a reason for doing so. Confessing may remove the person's guilty feelings, making him feel better, or it may reduce the amount of stress the person is subjected to while trying to maintain a lie.

There must be an incentive to exposing oneself to adverse actions or punishment.

The deceiver must believe that you know he is lying; you must have pointed out enough inconsistencies in his story that he doesn't believe he can get away with lying any further.

Interrogators should convince the person that they have proof of the person's guilt, and that the only option the person has left is to confess, thereby alleviating the stress of continuing to lie, and moving forward.

Reasons for Denials:

> Fear of Prosecution
> Fear of Being Fired
> Fear of Embarrassment
> Fear of Restitution
> Fear for their own or another's safety

People confess when the perceived benefits of a confessing outweigh the perceived consequences.

Over time, the denials and resolve of a truthful person

will increase, while a deceptive person's denials decrease.

Prior to confessing, the liar may present obstacles/denials, followed by attempts to bargain, or questions that test the waters, such as, *"What would happen to me if I did do it?"*

Your response should be, *"Would you rather deal with someone who has admitted to making a mistake, or with someone who continues to lie to you, even when you know the truth?"*

In the 'Theme Development' stage, you provide the subject with a rationalization or justification for the person's actions, which the person will buy into.

The 'Theme' is usually constructed out of motivations or minimizations the person expressed during the interview.

The justification does not have to be something the liar believes, you just need to convince him that you believe it, so he/she can save face.

In the 'Theme Development' stage you might blame the victim, blame stress, or anything else as a justification for the person's actions. Minimize and rationalize the person's actions, and find a way for the person to save face.

Next you will provide the 'Alternative Question', which accuses the person of the behavior, but also provides a rationalization for it – an incentive to confess to the act while still allowing the person to save face.

In Behavioral Modification, the operator seeks to reward desired behavior; the same is true during interviews/interrogations.

If you want a person to continue to be truthful, thank him/her for admitting to 'their mistake', and complement their willingness and courage to do so.

Next, ask the person to tell you what really happened. At this point you are seeking to corroborate the truth while still looking for signs of deception. The confession must be corroborated so that it is usable.

Bibliography

Charles R. Swanson, 1999, 'Criminal Investigation', McGraw-Hill

Christopher Dillingham, 2008, 'Dissecting Pinocchio: How to Detect Deception in Business, Life, and Love, iUniverse Inc.

David E. Zulawski, 1992, 'Practical Aspects of Interview and Interrogation', CRC Press

David Matsumoto, 2012, 'Nonverbal Communication: Science and Applications', Sage Publishing

George K. Simon PhD, 'In Sheep's Clothing: Understanding and Dealing with Manipulative People', 2010, Parkhurst Brothers

Humintell, 2011, 'Evaluating Truthfulness and Detecting Deception', Matsumoto Method Workshop

John R. Schafer, Ph.D., 2008, 'Psychological Narrative Analysis: A Professional Method to Detect Deception in Written and Oral Communication',

KLETC, 2011 'Interviews, Body Language, Verbal Cues and Eye Accessing Techniques for Detecting Deception', KS Law Enforcement Training Center

Mark McClish, 2012, 'Don't Be Deceived: The definitive book on Detecting Deception' Marpa Group

Paul Ekman, 2013, 'Telling Lies: Clue to Deceit in the Marketplace, Politics, and Marriage', W.W. Norton & Company

- About the Author -

Daniel E. Loeb is a graduate of American Military University, where he earned a Master of Arts degree in Homeland Security, and a Graduate Certificate in Terrorism Studies. He has a Bachelor of Science in Psychology, and an Associate of Allied Science in Airway Science. Sergeant Loeb also serves as a Sexual Assault Prevention and Response Coordinator Victim's Advocate. He volunteers as a Law Enforcement Officer, and is a member of the Community Emergency Response Team in his local community. Sergeant Loeb's served two tours in Iraq, and during his latest deployment authored and instructed a course in Close Quarters Combat to America's warfighters. He is a Black Belt in Jujitsu, a Defensive Tactics Instructor (for law enforcement), and was a registered coach with USA Boxing. Daniel Loeb is the author of several books. He is a Christian, a Father, a Scholar,   a   Teacher,   and   a   Patriot. **www.dwellwithprudence.com**

HANDS TO WAR

Fighting, Weapons, and Self-Defense for Christian Families

'Hands to War' is a self-defense book for Christian families. The book clarifies misconceptions some Christians might have regarding their right/obligation to defend themselves, and their duty to protect their families. The book teaches the Martial Arts, Boxing, Fencing, and Close Quarters Combat in order to produce a well rounded fighter capable of adapting to any situation. After learning the basics of the different fighting styles, the reader is taught how to easily master weapons such as the Knife, Sword, Sai, Nunchaka, and Tonfa – by building upon the skills they have already learned. The use of handguns in home defense is also covered. An entire chapter is dedicated to the Use of Force and the Inherent Right of Self-Defense. This book provides information on becoming a hard-target against terrorists and criminals. It teaches Christian self-defense principles combined with real world self-defense skills that the author taught to America's war fighters in a combat zone.

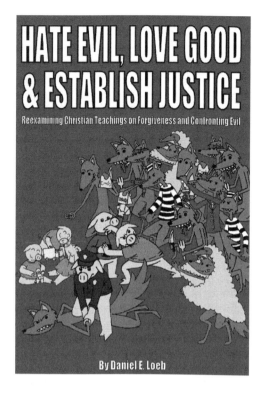

HATE EVIL, LOVE GOOD & ESTABLISH JUSTICE

Reexamining Christian Teachings on Forgiveness and Confronting Evil

By Daniel E. Loeb

Hate Evil, Love Good, & Establish Justice: Reexamining Christian Teachings on Forgiveness and Confronting Evil - takes a deeper look at Christian teachings that may be misconstrued, taken for granted, or only understood superficially. This book seeks to understand what the Bible teaches Christians in regards to their interactions with evil. It endeavors to determine whether or not Christians are obligated to love and forgive everyone, or if certain evildoers and certain sins should not be forgiven. Do parents need to forgive the murderer of their child, or do victims of other violent crimes need forgive their attackers? Does the Bible permit Christians to hate such people? Are there limits to who you are required to forgive? Are there some people that you should not reach out to or pray for? Did Jesus forgive everyone? This book deals with how Christians are to respond to evil. It explores forgivable and unforgivable sins, and includes Bible studies on lying and rape.

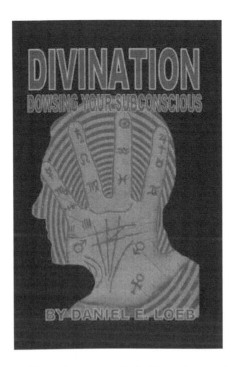

Divination - Dowsing your Sub-Conscious - teaches you how to gain information from your sub-conscious mind through Ideomotor Response, Tarot Cards, and Palmistry. Pendulum and Dowsing rod construction and use are also covered. Along with explaining how these processes work the author also covers the moral, ethical, and religious aspects of divination. This book is a valuable resource for parents who find their children experimenting with the occult and wish to have enough information available to have a rational debate. This book contains a thorough Bible study on divination providing the interested party with a complete understanding of the techniques and the Biblical view of practitioners. Dream interpretation and prophecy are also covered to explore the differences between divination, revelation, and personal intuition. Learning to use your intuition successfully can be a valuable tool in your life, but along with it comes additional responsibility.

Be Ye Transformed

Christianity, Hypnosis, and Behavioral Modification

By Daniel E. Loeb

Don't Wait Providence Publishing

***Be Ye Transformed: Christianity, Hypnosis, and Behavioral
Modification*** - So, you have decided become a Christian. Now
what do you do? When you become a Christian you become a
new creation, and the entire Christian faith is judged by your
actions. The Bible provides specific standards that Christians are
to live by. Behavioral Modification is of key importance to both
new and mature Christians. This book explores behavioral
modification, willpower, and leadership from a Biblical
perspective, and also covers the techniques used by man. This
book teaches how to use hypnosis in conjunction with other
techniques to assist you in modifying your behavior. This is a
comprehensive study of techniques of motivation and mental
influence. Some topics covered are: Hypnosis, Spirit vs. Flesh,
Leadership, Classical and Operant Conditioning, Aversion
Therapy, Systematic Desensitization, Implosion Therapy,
Motivation, Conflict Resolution, Weight loss, Smoking
Cessation, Power Learning, Subliminal Messages, Propaganda,
Logical Fallacies, Brainwashing, Mind Control, and a study of
the Trinity.

Rape and Sexual Assault

Awareness, Prevention, Defense
Response, and Recovery

This book will cover the following topics: Awareness, Prevention, Defense, Response, and Recovery from Rape, Sexual Assault, and/or Child Sexual Abuse. These topics are unpleasant to think about, but regrettably, the dangers they represent, and the impact/devastation caused in the lives of the victims of these crimes, necessitates the urgent need to discuss these topics, and to seriously contemplate the information.

THE QABALAH A. D.
THE CHRISTIAN KABBALAH

The word, 'Qabalah' means, 'to receive.' It is a system of studying 10 different names/attributes of God, and serves as a graphical aid to assist the reader in understanding the mysteries of God. This book is a collection of Bible studies on the 10 names/attributes of God, and the 22 Tarot Cards associated with the connecting paths. It is intended to assist the reader in understanding the nature of God, the mysteries of the Bible, and the path to salvation and spiritual growth. It builds on the efforts of Jewish Mystics and the Hermetic Orders in order to produce a completed version of the Qabalah – based solely on scripture taken from the Torah, Septuagint, and the New Testament of the Bible. The author spent over 15 years writing this book. Some of the chapters could not be written until the author, 'received' a greater understanding of the content, and advanced in his own spiritual journey. The accumulation of his efforts produced a scripturally sound and definitive work on the Christian Qabalah. This book is not merely the opinions of the author – or other men – regarding the different aspects of the Qabalah, but is a collection of scripture, painstakingly aligned with the different areas of the Qabalah, in order to produce studies that are truly inspired by God. Other works on the Christian Kabbalah merely provide short introductions to the concept of adding Christian principles to the Kabbalah. This book is The Christian Kabbalah.

By Daniel E. Loeb, M.A.

Live with Honor

Biblical Principles for Success in a World of Unbelievers

Behold, today I set before you a choice between good and evil, and life and death

This book is for to young adults who are just starting out in the world and for adults who have already entered the workforce. It is meant to serve as a guidebook to life, and to assist the reader in navigating a world filled with unbelievers. It is ideal for young adults who are first leaving home, going to college, or entering the workforce. It will help prepare the reader to go forth into a world filled with wolves, and to interact with nonbelievers productively. The author shares his experiences combined with relevant Biblical principles in order to help Christians successfully navigate a dangerous world and to assist them in finding success and happiness in life while in situations where they are unequally yoked with unbelievers. The author discusses honor and shares the concepts that have worked for him in order to succeed in various aspects of life, while maintaining a sense of honor, and by not compromising one's Christian values/virtues. The book answers tough questions regarding the meaning of life, good and evil, and understanding God. It assist the reader defining success, establishing priorities, examining human nature, and then provides principles/concepts to assist the reader in living a life with honor in an unbelieving world.

19527973R00044

Made in the USA
San Bernardino, CA
02 March 2015